Some bones and a story

Some bones and a story
by Alice Major

Wolsak and Wynn . Toronto

© Alice Major, 2001

All rights reserved. No part of this book may be reproduced or transmitted in any form, by any means, electronic or mechanical, without permission in writing from the publisher, except by a reviewer who may quote brief passages in a review. In case of photocopying or other reprographic copying, a licence is required from CANCOPY (Canadian Copyright Licensing Agency), One Yonge Street, Suite 1900, Toronto, ON, CANADA M5E 1E5.

Typeset in Galliard, printed in Canada by
The Coach House Printing Company, Toronto.

Cover art: © Colleen Philippi – *We have taken such a serpentine path* (detail), 1995
Cover design: Coach House
Author's photograph by Robert Chelmick, chelmick.com
Some of these poems have appeared in *Descant, Other Voices, Vintage '39, Hawthorne Anthology, 1996, Stand Magazine* (UK). An excerpt from "Saint Marina" was published in *Going it alone: Plays by women for solo performance* (Winnipeg, Nuage Editions, 1997). "Saint Marina" was a finalist in *Stand Magazine*'s long poem competition, 1996. "Saint Marina" and "Saint Scholastica" also appeared in the chapbook, *Complete within herself,* published by Reference West (Victoria, 1997).

The publishers gratefully acknowledge the support of the Canada Council for the Arts and the Ontario Arts Council.

Wolsak and Wynn Publishers Ltd.
192 Spadina Avenue
Toronto, ON
Canada M5T 2C2

National Library of Canada Cataloguing in Publication Data

Major, Alice, 1949-
      Some bones and a story

Poems.
ISBN 0-919897-74-6

I. Title.

PS8576.A515S65 2001   C811'.54   C2001-930593-1
PR9199.3.M346S65 2001

For three Marys of my family:
Mary Matheson – my mother
Mary Duffy – Granny
Mary Doran – Nanna

and for my sister, Carol

CONTENTS

Saint Catherine, in dispute   9

Saint Marina   11

Saint Pelagia   19

Saint Brigid and the blind nun, Dara   21

Saint Anne teaches her daughter to read   23

Saint Martha and the dragon   27

The Blessed Veronica and the Holy Family   33

The Saint's daughter   35

The Blessed Louisa Albertoni, widow   41

Saint Xene   43

Saint Paul, questioned   45

A supplication to Saint Anorexia   46

The cuckoo chick   47

Wilgefortis   51

Possessed by gravity   53

Saint Scholastica   60

Afterword   69

SAINT CATHERINE IN DISPUTE

*Saint Catherine, whose cult has been widespread and popular since the
ninth century, was removed from the official calendar in 1969. Her
feast day was suppressed because the church concluded there is insufficient
historical evidence of her existence.*

What was I then for a thousand years?
Just some bones and a story?

True, there were so many martyred virgins,
our stories splintering light like facets
of some whole that people needed.
All the Agathas, Eulalias and Agneses –
all the beautiful, chaste, intractable
objects of lust. All the breasts cut off and eyes
plucked out and throats pierced with spears.
No doubt it was excessive.

But that's not why you expunged me
from approved memory.

My story –
     *Catherine, intelligent and highborn
     lady of Egypt, pirated away to Rome.*

     *To tear away the Christian shield
     she raised around her beautiful body,
     the emperor pitted her against
     fifty pagan philosophers.*

     She converted every one of them.

But I don't convince you – you sifters
and squeezers who put me through the sieve
of 'historical accuracy,' and press and press,
until something you call truth drops through.
A clear and uncontaminated jelly.
While all the fecund detail of legend
is left behind, all the skins and stems and core.

Narrow-sighted, eyes squinting, tongues
clamped to one side in concentration,
you try to poke one black thread
through a fine needle, while all around you
hangs the vast, unwieldy arras
of belief, stiff with embroidery.

My story –
> *When she would not bend, they tried*
> *to break her on a wheel cruel*
> *with knives. The fierce apparatus*
> *flew apart in pieces, would not harm her.*

This was the tale people believed in,
prayed inside, drew to themselves
like the cloth woven so fine it slips
through the tiniest of gold rings.
It was real enough for Joan of Arc
to wear beneath her armour, but not for you.

My story –
> *she bled milk when she died.*

Only grey dishwater would drip
from your veins, you cleaners and tidiers,
scrubbing at the tales and graffiti of centuries
scribbled on the church's foundation. Ignoring
how your detergent faith erodes
something more than story.

SAINT MARINA

A woman disguised as a monk, accused of fathering the child of an innkeeper's daughter. She was punished for this "sin" by being sent to live outside the monastery gates for some years before returning. Her sex was discovered only after her death.

I. Why did I turn myself into a man?

They ask me that – all those young
women kneeling in the chapel
by my reliquary. Through the rattle
of censer chains, through the aves sung

at evensong, they make up stories.
"A young man you loved? A romance?
A handsome saint who wouldn't glance
at you – a lover meshed in the glories

of God? And you could not bear to part
from him. You shaped vows with your lips,
distilled your tears to worship,
hid your sex along with your heart."

Other maids make other tales of me.
How I must have loathed the distaff
twisting, the empty women's chaff
and clothed myself in breeches, gallantly.

Or some, looking neither left nor right,
but straight down into their hands
ask, "Why a monastery? Did it stand
surety for you? Was it flight

from some disturbing passion? Did you
feel you were a man in other ways?"
The stories rise and cluster in the nave,
dissolve in murmurs. None of them is true

> *They don't believe me when I say it wasn't*
> *anything so simple or so complicated.*
> *Not everything is shaped*
> *by the flesh between our thighs*
> > *There are*

other things – the cool stink of water
in a leather cup after labour in the fields.
The vellum silence of a line of gold
shaping into flowers, into fruit.

All this piling up of stones. Male here.
Female over there. It didn't matter
to me. I ate meat when I could get it,
or porridge, sat straining
over the hole to the cess-pit.
Slept. Worked. It was enough
to fill a life, enough to stuff
under a pillow at night
and dream about.

But still they press. *Why?*
Why? Until in irritation I might say
"Yes. I didn't want to be
with women in their whispering gowns.
They disturbed my peace."

But that's not it, really. It was
just the place life took me
– a square, dark, silent person
who sat listening to
a dry, distant thunder.

II. Childhood

Oh, yes, all those infant saints
and tales of holy precocity.
Miracle babies who wouldn't taint
their lips with food on Friday

or tiny girls who lisped, dove-eyed
and devout, to visiting bishops –
offering themselves as little brides
of Christ, young communion cups.

> *The fact is, I recall*
> *little of my childhood. Nor can*
> *anyone else. My mother died young.*

> *In the single memory of her I clasp*
> *like a saint's finger-bone in a casket,*
> *I am sitting, elevated, in a wooden chair*
> *Somewhere, to my left, a fire*
> *and my hands full with a cup*
> *of sweet milk. My mother's hand nearby,*
> *steadying. I feel it is worth all my small life*
> *to keep the milk unspilled.*

The monastery always there
at my shoulder, a paved courtyard
behind high walls, a well in the centre.

My father in his grief retired there,
took me too – for lack of anywhere else
to put me. Pretended I was a boy.

That suited me well enough. The place
was safe. I liked the smell of stables
and the incense and the sour bite of wine
held to my lips in a metal cup.
It helped to take away the sad taste
of milk.

13

III. When I heard God

This at least was granted me.
No lightning. No heaven opened radiantly,
no revelation of gems, no choired stairs
of coral and chrysoprase ascending to the stars.
No mounting song, no angels' rapture, no bliss
of seraphim.

I did not pray for visions such as this
while bent, stroking ink on the holy pages,
following the curve, the indivisible edges
of the great letter "O".
And my eyes were never opened so.

*It came as a voice that spoke my name
intimately, at my shoulder. My
name. The one my mother called me by.*

Only my name. God's voice said nothing
else. No commandments. But
as I raised my head from my work
I knew

that I was
growing, thrusting
down
into soil,
driving a taproot
down
to ground water
drawing up sap
to hold   within
my body.

I had become green vessel, trunk of tree
leading to the wander of branches.
From me came the grained articulation
of the wooden bench, the curved shaft
and iridescent, interlacing barbules
of the feather pen, the flourish of letters
on the shaped page.

It was a great blessing. I held the memory
inside myself, as if it were a child
in its sac of liquid. It moved and stirred
within me, all my life.

IV. The false accusation

Sex, again. There's no escaping its clutch
in all the stories that tumble and cling
around me, like sparrows twittering
in the marshy gloom that fills the church.

You might expect that I'd have laughed aloud.
But my first reaction was surprise –
a crazy instant of believing in her lie,
as she swung her finger at me, in the crowd

that gawked in the courtyard of the monastery.
She cowered from her father's rough threat
and raised arm. Cried, "Him! Him!" The abbot
looked relieved. The others looked curiously

at me. And I wondered for a moment who I was.
As though part of me had dried up, blown
off by the rough, warm wind. As though a stone
flung by a blind hand had left me dazed.

> *Up to that instant*
> *I had no*
> *connection with her.*
> *All she needed at that moment*
> *was some – any – other.*
> *They could not let her be complete*
> *within herself.*

She died in childbirth, and the infant with her.
When I heard, I felt an unexpected pang – almost
as if, indeed, I'd lost a son.

V. The discovery

At last, death. Ordinary as water
drying on the paving stones
where I fell. A gasp and a going away.

Later, wrapping me for burial, they discovered
what I had almost forgotten. That fold of flesh,
that soft labial buckle by which I should have been
fastened somewhere else.

Gasps, then! A novice sent scampering
for the abbot, while the brothers waited with
their basins and shroud linen, wondering
desperately – how could they have knelt
or sat or laboured beside me
all those years and not known? It rocked
some central tenet of the faith they held.

The abbot sweeping in. The cloth delicately drawn
aside. The bent heads, the murmuring.
The potential for scandal summed up
in one irritated command. "No one
must know."

> *Of course the story sifted*
> *through the monastery walls.*
> *Ownerless, drifting thistledown*
> *sprouting in strange places*
> *until they began to call on me as saint.*

The wonder of it was –
not that I was so blessed or
so holy. Simply
that I was in the wrong place.

VI. Inside the reliquary

My bones. A white assortment.
The curved, clubbed femur, the carpels
like ivory game-pieces, the round orbit
of eye-bone. A cask a little bigger
than a cutlery drawer, that holds only
dry things now.

This: my gift back to the church,
which needs such stones to build on –
enough of earth to rise from
the great, swamping seacoast.

What the church gave me:
a thimbleful of liquid to hold
in my flesh as a breast holds milk.
Water enough to fill
a cup, a quill, a human soul.
It was all I asked. It was
enough.

SAINT PELAGIA

*"Pelagia the Penitent," a notoriously licentious dancing girl, was
converted after hearing a sermon by Bishop Nonnus of Edessa. Scholars
have suggested her legend is a Christianizing of Aphrodite or Venus.*

She lived in Antioch – city of the crossroads,
city of olives and the flat scent of dung
two days' journey from the sea. They told stories
of her dancing, of how her limbs made love
to empty air until men could imagine
the roundness of arms, the sympathy of skin,
until they could taste the ocean salt beneath
her tongue. Pelagia, Aphrodite's daughter,
named for the sea. Although the bishops
called her other names.

The people called her "Margarito"
for the fineness of her pearls, round and pale
as Aphrodite's ankle, pierced and strung with thread.
In the speech of the market place,
such perforated pearls are called a different name
than unpierced, virgin stones.

In the church, the bishop told his stories –
how the twelve gates of the holy city
were all pearls and how the saints went in and out,
corporeal bodies turned as light as air.
He turned his words towards Pelagia,
penetrated her with rapture – words, breath,
aspiration.

She embraced his tales – incorporated
their parchment pledges with the wafer
that sucked moisture from her tongue. She turned
inland, renounced her liquid element.
The stories say she clothed herself as a man,
lived solitary on the mount of olives, died
a long way from the sea.

She left the church her wealth, her perforated
pearls. Perhaps the bishop set them in a sacramental cup
made to hold that salt liquid, blood,
the taste of word made flesh.

SAINT BRIGID AND THE BLIND NUN DARA

Ireland's beloved St Brigid founded the abbey of Kildare ("Kil-dara," the Church of the Oak). Many legends and miracles attributed to her are conflated with stories of the Celtic goddess Brigid, associated with fire, spring and the returning sun.

Blind from birth, the poor woman, and one
given to thinking much about the glories.
But neat and handy about her duties.
Her habit clean and soft as wheat flour,
as she sat beside me on the hill beyond the abbey
of Kil-dara, in the cool twilight.

The end of May it was, and the sun stepping
towards its high point on the dais of the year.
Oh, the splendour of it setting in the west
that evening. A rosy ring of cloud
made cushions for the Hesperus star.
White rowan blossom glimmered pale
in the dusk. Such mild and winning evenings are
rare in this world.

But Dara did not even sniff the air, sharp
with the catch-throat scent of rowan. She
talked of Paradise instead, and her thirst
for Jesus Christ. The longing in her voice
trembled like new milk in the pail.

All night we talked together, about what was good
in this life and the next. And all that short night,
the Milky Way was draped and pegged with stars,
like angels' washing hung to dry on fields
of heaven. And then the sky began to lighten
and the sun got up – a brass ball shining
its heart out – and the dew white and sheer
as the veil of our lady lying on the grass.

It saddened me to know that Dara couldn't see it.
Such a miracle of a dawn seemed reason enough
for another miracle. So I bowed my head,
prayed to the source of all brightness,
then passed my hand over her eyes.

Her darkness cleared, and she looked for a while
on the lovely whole. But then she turned to me
and said, "Close my eyes again, mother,
for when the world is so visible to the eyes
God is seen less clearly by the soul."

Well, the dear woman. What could I do?
Though I longed to shake her and say
"God lives in this world too, Dara. Don't
turn up your nose at the cup he offers here."

But hush there. Who was I to pull her
like a winkle from its shell? I only prayed for her again,
and saw her eyes go blind once more. I helped her
to her feet and we made our way
through the bright morning.

SAINT ANNE TEACHES HER DAUGHTER TO READ

I see her so clearly still. Her child's lips
budding around the letter *bet.*
"Bih. Bih. Bih." Sending little kisses
to the crackled page.

Her favourite letters were the sibilants.
"S ... samach ... for *sefer,"* she would hiss
like a cheerful little snake, then clench her teeth
to whisper, *"Sh ... shin ...* for *shabbas."*

Her hair under my hand straight and smooth
as the fine cloth of a torah cover. She wore
the serious precocity that often comes
to late-in-life children, as though somehow
they've been living here beside you
all these years – in your body, learning,
listening in.

And something beyond love would turn in my gut,
something beyond pride. Though I was filled
with love and pride till it hurt like a stopped vein.
But something even more – a fierce longing
for her to be more real, more solid even
than she was, standing by my knee. As though
I feared that she might slip away again
to the realm of might-have-been.

Her father acquiesced in teaching her,
although he blamed me for it after.
He was not a lettered man himself.
So few were. But he doted on her,
and she loved to trace her letters
in the brown-scrolled dust for him.
"Samech, peh, resh, mem. That spells
sippurim – stories, papa.
Tell me one."

She grew up my heart's delight – a solid girl
like me, with a square, sweet face and a gravity
about her, as though she pulled the planet
a little way towards her when she walked.

And then it all went wrong.

The times were restless, people went
a little crazy, seeking something to hang
their lives on. Some young people
from the village and others from the hills
would gather in the corner places
where young people argue earnestly
about how things should change.

And Mary one of the leaders, one
who drew the others. Not so pretty
as some other girls, but she had
so much to say – her words fluent
and impassioned as though
she read them straight from the ciphered sky.
She would come home through the sage scent
of those summer evenings, breathing deeply,
and tell me all about it – who said what,
and who had not considered
that cause or this consequence.

And then a few weeks when she seemed
a little silent, as though she was turning over
some new story in her head. But still
my helpful girl, attentive to her chores. Until
the night when she abruptly came to us and said
she had to marry Joseph. Had to. For no reason
she would tell us.

She pulled a curtain over my dismay
and hid behind it. Joseph standing in the shadows
at the back of the room, where he stayed
as long as I knew him, a slightly sullen presence.
Mary stonily denying she was pregnant.

24

Her father didn't see it as disaster.
Daughters marry. She was of that age,
at least had chosen someone
from a family we knew, someone
who wouldn't take her away. What
more did I want?

How could I say?

True, life settled quietly, like ink drying
on familiar verses of the psalms.
I had her near. The ferment that pulled
so many of her friends away to the hills,
to dip their heads in crazy fountains
passed us by. For that time,
at least. I would visit her and find
a competent young mother
with high standards of housekeeping.

And I would find her teaching
the little one to read. *"Aleph, bet ..."*

Yes, I loved him too. The bright intelligence
of his little face, his way of asking
unexpected questions, large and ponderous
as the pentateuch. But as he learned to talk, she
seemed to fall more silent. She pondered things
but spoke of them less often.

Sometimes, I'd see a flicker of her old self
in him – her ardent ideas, her love of stories,
the poet's rhythm in his words, read from a sky
so full of potential. She was there, a little.

She is not there in the giant canvases,
the painted images – fair-haired, ethereal,
feet in the clouds. Those are not
pictures of my Mary. Nor can she be found
in the copied gospels or the tales they tell.
There, she is no more than a shadow
in the foreground, a sheet of pale vellum
from which his words are lifted.

I wanted *her* words written down. I wanted
her to remain real, to pull the parchment earth
towards her and inscribe it with her alphabet
of illuminated letters. *Resh. Aleph. Shin.*
Rash – "Beginning."

I wanted it to be my daughter,
not her son.

SAINT MARTHA AND THE DRAGON

> *In Provençal legend, Mary, Martha and their brother Lazarus fled the*
> *Holy Land after the crucifixion, made their way to the Rhone estuary*
> *and evangelized the area around Marseilles. Lazarus became first*
> *bishop of Marseilles. Mary retired to spend thirty years in the wilderness,*
> *while Martha is said to have subdued a dragon and led it to Arles.*

I. Bethany

In the first place
we were sisters.

And Mary was as happy to play house
as I. Two little girls in Bethany
mapping out imaginary rooms
with olive twigs and fragrant sprigs
of rosemary. Industrious
in the courtyard dust, we were supervised
by the house lizards – the tiny ones
that curled in my hand
and smelled like clay pots, baking.

Mary was the one who said
Now you come to the door
and I'll invite you in for cakes.

And Lazarus, still thumb-in-the-mouth,
crying because he expected
real cake.

II. The kitchen

Yes, I'd get exasperated at the girl,
curled on the cushions, arguing fiercely
that the rich man should get into Paradise.
Why shouldn't he? she'd demand.
That's just not fair.
You tell me riches are a load to shed.
Then you say the man with the coins
must use them well. Make up your mind.

While I was interrogating chicken feathers
and debating nice points with the pots –
how much grain would be needed
to fill those chattering mouths.

I wanted to be in there too, hearing
about the crowds in restless Jerusalem.
But someone had to think of dinner
for those poor men who'd walked
the length of Samaria. Pretend cake
wouldn't do.

So I'd flick a lizard tongue at her.
And she'd swing the shutter of her hair
between us and ask another question.

III. The ointment

You know that it was mine. I had
a reputation for it, even then.
For mixing balms and lotions, perfumes
to make sick people think of crocuses
reviving the weary air
after winter's drought of scent.

I loved the art of it, the mingling
of gum arabic and oil of amber
with white threads of gum-dragon
that I gathered in the wild hill country
from low, thorny bushes.

There was gum-dragon in
that ointment. The jar I gave to Mary
to soothe on his raw skin. All three
of us cried out to see his cracked
and blistered feet. He came so far
to heal our brother and could not
heal himself.

And while we wept, the house was filled
with the odour.

IV. Provence

That foreign country smelled of sea-mud
and salt. The years went by, wearing
their path to our door.

All the feet that came to us,
all the seekers and penitents and
visiting bishops. All the prayers
and sermons, all the mouths
that chattered and had to be fed.
Mary gone away and Lazarus meshed
in the grating of the church. The healer
was gone from us and we quarrelled
over how to heal ourselves.

It was a great dragon winding
in and out of the house, and me alone
to feed its ever-lengthening gut.

That worm was eating up my life,
and one day, at last, I told myself
"The worms will have enough of you
all too soon."

So I came away to find a place
where the scent of rosemary blows
through my window
and the bread can rise in peace.

V. The hermitage

I hear tales of Mary in the wilderness.
They say she's nourished on celestial food
and carried up to heaven daily
by angels.

And have to laugh. That's where they all
think food comes from – that magic cook-pot
in the sky. While someone else is off
chopping garlic and squeezing lemons
to sustain the heavenly illusion.

          She lives
a long way off. I visit when I can.
She is careless of herself
so I take dried fruit and strips
of fish, jars of sour-bitten plums.

Last time, I also took a balm to soothe
the rubs and blisters raised
by the rough garments she wears
so passionately and
so absent-mindedly.

She drew her hair aside to let me
spread lotion on her frail shoulders,
and bent forward from the waist.

I patted oil on her back – so slight. So
unexpectedly familiar. Words
uncoiled suddenly, a phrase
alive in my inner ear:

    My
    little
    sister

As though the past
was resurrected – whole and pungent
from lavender.

Tears stung me
as if I breathed through smoke
and my throat ached
as I inhaled
the dragon's
perfumed
breath.

BLESSED VERONICA AND THE HOLY FAMILY

We all have our talent
to lay at the feet of the Church
And mine was tears.

Well, you couldn't expect scholarship
or rich gifts to the convent.
Not from a family like mine. My father,
a tinsmith, did his best for us,
but couldn't sell a pot without
pointing out the smallest dent in it
– and never mention its good qualities.

I felt the slight of it, not so much
as a brass cup to gift the convent with
when I took the veil. But then I thought
any woman can cry, that's
what the men say anyway. So I decided
to make a virtue of it.

I'd kneel and tuck my hands
together and think of ... oh, Mary
and the Holy Family and Saint Joseph
maybe like my own father just
hammering away at life when no one
gave him much respect –
and there I'd go. Tears simmering over
and down my cheeks.

I could keep it up for hours, until the floor
looked like a careless baptism. It was
quite a mark of holy favour for the convent.

Once, just for the measuring, they held a bowl
under my chin. The novices took turns
to hold it while I prayed and thought
of Mary washing out His precious
swaddling clothes, until her hands were cracked
and raw as my poor sister's with her five
children, or that sweet Child without a toy to play with
drawing patterns in the dust on the road to Egypt –
and on I flowed.

A whole quart in that bowl
by vespers. I felt a little
lightheaded after, when they showed
it to me. All that tribute
from my poor old eyes. The liquid
was thicker than water, but clear
and deep enough for the Christ-fish
to swim in.

Now, there's ways and ways of holiness
and you might think a pot of salt water
isn't much. But show me any pope
who's done the same. The stories swam
through the country around Binasco, bringing
such honour to my family. "Yes, that's our
Veronica," they say. "She always had the gift."

THE SAINT'S DAUGHTER

The first decade

God was everywhere.
I peed as quiet as I could in the night-pot
not to interrupt his holy thoughts. Everywhere.

In the kitchen with my mother,
in her beads clicking
paternoster paternoster paternoster.
He lived in my chest, beside my rosy heart,
knew I wanted a doll. Told me not to.

God everywhere and Mama
not wanting anything. Holding a spoon to her lips
not sipping, putting it down.

The rose bush at the door, all thorns.
I held a tiny bud on my lips, a pink offering.
Perhaps God's mother would come to the gate,
take rosebuds from my mouth to make a chaplet.
She did that for the young monk in the tale.

God everywhere and all my dead brothers and sisters,
their names pattering like mice in a drawer.
        Ring a round a rosy ...
and they all fell down, scattered beads,
me the last one clinging to the string.

They crowded in my room at night. I lay breathless,
not to draw them to me. *Shhh, I* told the kitten
Hold still. But he wiggled free of me,
leapt onto the window sill, looking out.

Mama, Mama, I shouted and she came
like an angel. *There, there.* She stroked my hair.
*Just a dream. Say your prayer. Jesus keeps
you safe.* As she stared out the window.
God and mama and the cat
seeing in the dark. I shut my eyes.

The second decade

Confirmation. The bishop's hands
a tickle on my hair. I dangled in anticipation
waiting for the holy ghost to swell inside me,
trembled at my first communion,
afraid the wine would really taste like blood.
When the host touched my tongue, I expected
that I would start to shudder as Mama did,
as though she were a pot of boiling water.

But nothing happened. God was
behind the stained glass windows,
behind Mama's eyes.

Father's people gathered in the church porch
in their Sunday best. My rude and ruddy cousins
whooping around the yew trees.
The aunts muttering about my mother.

She was a pretty little thing when Albrecht married her.
But now she's skin and string.
            Dieter saw her stock-still in the street
            staring into the sky. The whole town will be laughing.
When did she begin to go this way?
            Oh, not long before her second son was stillborn.
How many?
            Eight, before this scrawny one, holding on
            long enough to reach communion.
You'd think her peasant breeding would be healthier.

. . .

Father was a fury brewing through the afternoon,
then crashing through the door. If the soup tureen
wasn't steaming on the table, if his chair wasn't pushed
in place, it was *Can't a man expect a decent meal*
and thumps and thunders. The cat and I sidled into corners.

Mama, calm as a candle, waited for the gusts to gutter out,
opened the shutters. *You've had a hard day*
she'd murmur. *What happened in the shop?*
And father would fume about the Damascus blade
that flew apart under his hammer, and the brute
who wouldn't pay for a fine scabbard. Mama
hushed and lullayed until Dada grabbed her hand
and gave a dry hiccup and said, *You're a good wife,*
Dorthea, too good for me. A saint.

                                And I would feel
awkward, as though Dada had become one of his own lumps
of battered steel, folded over and over. Only you couldn't hear
a clang of victory from Mama. Perhaps a little, muted bell
when she called us to our rosaries,
and Dada would grumble again and lumber
to his knees. While Mama prayed for those who spoke evil
and those in need and the people of the church
and the widow around the corner. While I felt myself drifting
off, growing distant, a speck becoming lost
in a vast sky.

The third decade

Then you left us, Mama. On your pilgrimage.

You had left so often, coaxing Father
to come with you. To see the relics at Cologne,
Aachen, Einseideln.

And this year was the Jubilee – all Christendom
crowding into Rome for penance and pardon
and the pope's blessing. Father was going with you
yet again, only he fell ill, his chest suddenly tight,
no room to swing the hammer.

Go, go, he told you. *You'll never rest unless ...*
He didn't finish. We watched you recede
down the road, pilgrim's scrip at your waist,
your pace increasing away from us.

And then Dada died. There was just time
enough to send a neighbour for the priest,
to hear my father say *Dorthea. Dorthea.*
She'll have Jesus Christ to comfort her.
A wistfulness, as though he'd lost you
to another man. For a moment, I dared
to hate you.

The fourth decade

You wanted to go away, Mama.
You spoke to me gently. What did I want
to do? Marriage?
                       I swung like a knotted cord
at a nun's waist. Who was there to marry?
No suitor brought me posies. Too thin. Too pale.
Too old. Too strange.

But not as strange as you, Mama. You shocked me,
describing how the sacrament affected you.
It left you with a leaping in your belly
like a fish, a fetus planted by a holy spouse,
shudders like the convulsions of climax.
I felt that I had caught you copulating.

We sold the house. I came dowered to this convent,
attached my sadness to its quiet string of rules.
And watched you detach
from this world. You went to Marienwerden.
Widowed, able at last to marry
the other.

They let you build a cell against the church wall –
a tiny room. Three windows. One opened onto the altar.
One out to the graveyard. One up to the sky.
Your name spread wings. Visitors came
for revelation and advice. Another man
wrote the story of your life and visions.

You lived a year in this way – prostrating your body
on the cold stone, adoring the host,
bearing your angel children.

Then they brought me word
of your death. A string snapped.
Ave. Ave. Ave
           rolling on the floor.

The fifth decade

I am older now than you were at your death,
Mama. You and Jesus off together in that vast sky.

I try to to love him, serve him for you.
But I am always wanting.
Mother abbess comforts me, threads
my pierced heart back on the string.
I return to my tasks like a cat, not knowing
whether I want in or out.

But I do know what
I want, Mama.
What I have wanted
all these years. What
I cannot stop
wanting, even when
I beg myself
to squeeze such
childish longing
aside, since God
is everywhere
and should fill up
all space.

I want you to want
me. To bend
and kiss the rosebuds
from my lips.

The Blessed Louisa Albertoni, Widow

"I'm leaving you well provided for, Louisa,"
he said, wheezing under the mound
of linen bedsheets, like a cook's bellows
puffing uselessly at a cooling fire.
We buried him in his fine brown coat
with the horn buttons, on a day of dark rain.
Oh, the weight of him going down. The faces
of the gravesmen, grimacing and sweating
as they lowered the box, stay with me.
And the heavy sound of clay clapping
thick oak.

So there I was. Widowed, and one
of the wealthiest women in the town.
I hardly knew what to do with it all.
And so many needs to fill, so many
suggestions. Young artists, short of fame
by the price of a few tubes of paint.
Mothers begging, their babies in the crook
of their arms. The blind and lame
common as straws in the square
after market day, and just as broken.
Who was to say who deserved what?

Until, in desperation, I thought of the loaves
and fishes. Everyone needs food, I said,
and ordered up a great load of flour
and set the maidservants to kneading
as if salvation depended on our fingers.

And when the bread was rising
for the second time, I tiptoed down
with a heavy purse of coins, to tuck
a farthing here, a florin there
into the dough. Then switched the pans
all round. Not even I would know
who received what. I gave the bread away,
trusting charity would fall like seed
in the furrows where it would be
most welcome.

"Well, the method works for God's word,"
I told the bishop when he came by
to scold me and tell me he could
help direct my future efforts. "Everyone
gets a share, and it most helps those
in greatest need."

So I gave everything away. Bun after bun,
pan after pan. Purse after purse.

'Til now I feel light as a loaf of good bread
swelling in the oven. Sometimes
I stand at a corner in the town and feel
my heart lifting until it seems my feet
are hardly near the ground.
And rapt, I think of angels coming for me
with wings as soft and white as risen bread,
and the fragrance of warm yeast going up.

SAINT XENE

They named me "piety" –
Eusebia. I was raised in courtyards
whose boundaries were marked
indelibly by decorum
and the domestic gods.

They chose a husband for me,
and the little girls gathered round
envious, as I was fitted
with the saffron wedding robes.
They chattered like the fire
on the hearth. *How many servants
will you have? When will you have
babies?*

My mother spoke tenderly to me.
Apprehensiveness was natural,
she said. Marriage would feel
a little strange at first, like new shoes.
But strangeness would pass away
quickly, when I took my place
in the precincts where matrons
map out their days. The name
I was to take was rich and honourable.
Cardea, goddess of door hinges,
would bless the comings and goings
of my family.

And because I was bred to piety
I turned obediently and watched
the flamen-coloured fabric swirl
around my sandals.

Until the night before the wedding.
The way my husband-to-be
clasped my hand, like the fibula
shaped into a golden knot
clasping his cloak.

I let myself through a side door.
It squeaked lightly in protest.
But I went out under the lintel
into the night shriven with stars,
found my way to the harbour
and a ship bound for Mylassa.
I learned to walk in bare feet
to sleep on the hard ground
beyond the precincts, found
another god and took the name
of "stranger."

SAINT PAUL, QUESTIONED

The women came in the evening's half-light,
their outlines blurred by hoods around their faces.

Who is this Mary? they asked. *This*
virgin called whore? This one
beloved of Christ? Where does she belong?

She is nothing, I told them. A misreading,
a dead end. And I showed them the bright light,
the straight, white, glorious road, the tiers
of men and angels pinnacled by God.

But, they said, *we have been told she is*
powerful, third part of trinity, the silence
of perfect wisdom.

I warned them against the attractions of heresy,
the seduction in shadows. I spoke of the beautiful
order, the loveliness of hierarchies stretching up.

But they continued to argue
with me, wilfully closed their eyes to the light.
They asked, *Is there nothing more than this for us?*
How do you explain the shadows cast by light?

Until I lost patience and told them, There is no need
to skulk in shadows when the light is there for all to see
and if silence is so perfect, then let a woman keep
silence in the church.

A SUPPLICATION TO SAINT ANOREXIA

Take this defect from me
that I may become perfect.
Strengthen me to purge this appetite,
this craving of body.

> *It lies just beyond this point, elusive*
> *will-o-wisp, the almost*
> *unachievable. It is a door so narrow*
> *few may pass through.*

Hone me to the slivered slenderness
of a knife blade. Lay my edge
to the throat of imperfection.

> *You have set the keen tip*
> *of desire in my veins.*
> *Fiercely I pare my gross*
> *flesh. Stubborn*
> *I close my stained lips.*

Keep this food from my mouth.
Take this cup from my lips.

THE CUCKOO CHICK

Her father settled her with us,
consigned her hand to mine as though he set
an egg in a nest. It lay tranquil in my palm –
smooth, white, faintly warm
against my rough old skin. "Welcome, daughter,"
I murmured, signed the blessing
between us.

A good girl from a good family. Pretty,
with a quick mind. Her father sighed
to leave her in the flock of novices.
"I could make a marriage for her
quick as you could dab a cross in the air,"
he murmured in the chattering hall at dinner.
"But she will not have it." His face
baffled, hurt beyond the simple loss
of a valued article for barter.

"She will be safe within our rule," I promised
watching her eager face, expecting
she would be one of the easy ones to care for
among this brood of orphan vocations.

. . .

Then became less sure. I would find her in the chapel
crouched below the crucifix – a fine new rood
of ebony and bronze presented to the convent
by her father. The artist has caught too well
the haggard, sagging agony.

She looks on it
as hers, as her peculiar inspiration.
It's the cruel holes she stares at,
unearthly appetite fledging in her face
until I send her to the garden or the barn
to think about life.

In the refectory, among the other open faces
she fasts – a mouthful of porridge on Fridays,
no more. She sits rapt and trembling
through the mass, takes the wafer on her tongue
like a greedy nestling – as if she would devour
the others' share as well.

I call her to my study. We talk of pain
and mortification, and how sometimes they conceal
a cavernous pride.

"Don't seek more than your share," I tell her.
"Yes, Christ suffered greatly.
But even He asked the bitter cup
be taken from him. Pain is not
for everyday wear." She nods obedient
for the moment, sips milk under my supervision.

But then I find her habit speckled with blood, her shoulders
striped from the scourge. I remonstrate again.
"I stand in place of a mother to you,"
I say. "Your mother orders
that you moderate excess."

But I am a sparrow mothering a cuckoo chick.
This gigantic holiness, this gaping beak
that demands to be filled.

The others do not help. The girls begin
to emulate her. We waste meals, and their strength.
Then the prelate on his fat pony, who visits
once a month. "You have a young saint there,"
he says. "All the villages around
are talking of this girl."

Dear God, what are we hatching?

. . .

And here we come to the lean days of Lent,
a late and frozen spring, my knees raw from the prie-dieu.

This morning's meal. The novices in rows.
And this wilful one sitting with an empty bowl.
I called her to me. Her pretty young plumpness
now strained and scrawny, her cheekbones
and neck muscles sharp below the skin.

"Why do you not eat?" I asked.
She dropped her eyes. *God told me*
she murmured, and the room ran with a current
carried on the sidelong slide of eyes.

This voice directs her to abstain from food
through Lent, she said – tells her to survive
on water and some herbs.

A rage rose in my throat, thickened my tongue.
I stood, felt my black robes shake, cawed at her
to fill her bowl and eat.

She spooned the porridge, gasping
as if a great beak forced grubs
down her throat. Turned and retched.
The kitchen cat appeared from nowhere,
stepped around the effluvium, sniffed,
slunk away.

I sent her to her cell, sent a sister with her –
phlegmatic Sister Angela, a woman unlikely to fall
into raptures. Ordered others to their duties.

Girls' voices a muted chorus as they left.
Wasn't her vomit sweet, like roses?
I needed a calmer voice to tell them
it smelled of undigested porridge, nothing more.

· · ·

I don't know who
to pray to.
Or for what.

Is it rage or fear that rattles
my chest as though my ribs were bars
on a cage? And beyond the bars,
this bird who hides in a thorn bush
and peers at me.

Dear lady of sparrows,
on my knees I gasp
supplication
for patience, for control
of my own shaking heart, for power
over myself, who have no power
over her. God save me, I want to clutch
claws in her shoulder, unlock her stubborn mouth and croak
Take. Eat.

WILGEFORTIS

Saint Wilgefortis, hear
my prayer. He's here again,
drunk and bashing round
the kitchen. The kids and I
shrinking, our stomachs
knotted like sheep gut
around sausage meat.
Can't I have this one space
free? Even in a prison,
don't the gaolers stay
outside your cell?

I hear it all the time. Neither prayers
nor people change much through the centuries.
I prayed like that myself – when my father
turned down his mouth, ordered me to wed
the King of Sicily. A strutting little lord.

And I prayed so hard for help they couldn't
ignore me. God replied by letting me
grow a beard. Probably thought it was funny.
Some joke, huh? As if that's what
I wanted – as if I'd said, "if you can't
beat 'em ..."

Sure, the Sicilian withdrew his suit.
My father so angry, he had me crucified –
rage gusting through him. When all I wanted
was a little peace and quiet in a convent
cell, somewhere.

So of course everyone cooled off
at last. Felt a bit stupid. Made me
a saint to say they were sorry. *Made*
me, as though I was a piece of plasticine
to stick up on the mantel.

51

Wilgefortis, hear my prayer.
Sometimes it's just the noise
that I can't stand. The pain
hardly matters. But the grumbling
sour as puke, then the shouts
like gunshots.

> Don't blame me if I appear in visions,
> subversive saint –
> if I stand there, radiant, my hands
> held out wide, my voice sweet
> and reassuring as I say:

Cut off his dick
Get the meat knife
Go for his balls

> You put me here, bearded,
> in your holy pantheon
> of rage.

POSSESSED BY GRAVITY

The Blessed Eustochium of Padua suffered throughout her life from episodes of 'possession' during which she mutilated herself or attacked others. In one of these fits, she climbed or flew up to the ceiling of the convent. By her death she had overcome these periods of violence.

Looking down on
their white faces
from the roof-beam.
Down at the gape
of the open bible, at
the long refectory
table spread
below me like a pit.

How did I come
to scramble up here?

The prioress was reading aloud.

Words throbbed in my head.
A great rage whirled me up, a wave
with foam spittle, flinging me – a fist
of beaten granite clutching for
the shore's rock-strewn breast

stranding me
here where
the roof beam
leaves the stone wall, leans out
over emptiness.

   . . .

They are calling me.
Come down, come down

I cannot come down. This is where I live.
      On one side, the lunge
into space, the vast vertigo of silence.

On the other, the bulk of matter,
the stone mountain, gravity added up
to the crippling weight of the world.

Between them,
a standing place,
narrow
as a pillar
in the desert.
Here I
exist, one cheek
pressed desperately
to the stone surface, the other
fanned by icy nothing.

How numb I am
from holding on.

. . .

if I say my prayers like a good girl
if I say my prayer
mother will let me
down, mother will stop
shaking me in mid-air   if I say my prayer
mother will stop shaking
will let me down from the table
will stop staring in my face
and shaking me   if I say my prayers like a good girl
she will let me
down will go
away somewhere   will stop hurting

. . .

I have tried to absolve
pain with emptiness,
emptiness with pain.

I set the knife's edge
on my skin, watch
it dent
like a pillow
under tension
from a cord.

Pull the knife
into the flesh.
A scratch at first,
beads on a thread,
a scarlet rosary.

Then I carve
deeper, needing.

The slivering blade
divides pain. One one side
the hurt of my body, the part
I can bear.

On the other, the ache
I cannot face, so entire
it has no beginning in space
or time. Pain, mother
of dark stars that emit no light,
but crush their children infinitely.

I do not want to die.
I only want the pain
to stop.

. . .

Come down, come down
the nuns call, like sirens
in black gowns, like my mother
calling me to her stone breast.

I loathe them.
They tied me to a pillar
and deserted me.
They say I am not safe
for myself or others.

The abbess with her white face
her long fingers like obedient snakes
curled around her crucifix.
Cut them off. Cover the black table
with red blood. Fill up the world.

· · ·

Come down. Come down.

I look into their narrow eyes.
I cannot read what their faces say.
Horror? Fear? Revulsion?

What can they know
of how I have to live.
For them, air spreads its calm wing overhead,
the ground unrolls its tranquil carpet from their feet.

They do not live
in this vertical hell
where god screams
in your face
like a mad-eyed gull. *You can fly
you can fly.*

I will drop like a stone.

· · ·

The prioress was reading aloud
from Revelations:
> *And to the woman were given two wings*
> *of a great eagle, that she might fly*
> *into the wilderness,   into her place,*
> *where she is nourished for a time*
> *and times, and half a time*
> *from the face of the serpent.*

I fly into my place, wingless.
I cling to the stone cliff.
The serpent wears my mother's face
suffused, screaming, spitting
a stream of poisoned milk.

        . . .

Come down, you'll hurt
yourself, they call.

But really they want me
just to go away.
Go and marry. We'll arrange
the dowry. Go
to another convent.

The abbess stands forward,
hushes the others.
Come down, Eustochium
she says gently.
Her face is clear and pale
as a candle flame, its shining edge
inserted into the transparent envelope
of air like a knife, keen and
bloodless.

The bible's white face stares up at me.
Come down, come down.

Hate is melting out of me,
like wax from a mould.
I am becoming, again,
a brittle cast and a void.

        . . .

When I die,
the cross I burned
on my soft breast
will be revealed.

I held the wire
in the candle flame
watched it turn red,
rage red. Touched

the wire to my skin.
Angry tooth.
Sharp suckling.

The pain, the waves like waves that leave
a swimmer gasping. Falling consciousness.
The strange, charred, charnel smell.

All the hurt drawn down
and cauterized.
My flesh bubbled
did not bleed.

That was the last time,
I promise, I promise.
I will not hurt you any more.

When my father and my
mother forsake me,
then God shall take me up.

        . . .

Now unto him that is able to keep me from falling ...

Saints set gravity at naught
all the time. Notaburga
hangs her sickle on the air, a temporary moon,
to keep the Sabbath holy.
Gudula scorns the gift of gilt-laced gloves,
leaves them floating, dispossessed, above the ground.

And Lucifer falls endlessly
into the abyss.

I do not ask so much
of God – do not ask to rise in the lightness of saints.

I ask only
not to fall.

SAINT SCHOLASTICA
*Twin sister of Saint Benedict of Nursia, who founded the abbey of
Monte Cassino on the site of Apollo's temple in the sixth century and
wrote the famous rule for monastic life.*

Vespers

The evening meal is set
on the table – dark bread a breviary
over which we bow our heads. And then you are set
on leaving.

          Benedict, my brother, my twin,
I ask you again to stay. There is a dark bread
rising in me, and rats gnaw it. Only a crust of time
is left on my plate. Grant me a wafer of yours,
one last night's communion.

How often have we met here, once a year,
halfway between our houses of religion,
to debate holy questions? Tonight, I crave
homelier things. To recollect
our whole-milk days in Nursia.
          Won't that gentle name
tempt you to stay?

Remember us – children,
twinned in our self-contained games?
Like apple pips, enclosed
in tough, translucent walls.

          Remember
how father would cut apples with his knife
for us to share? So sharp a blade
that when you held the halves together
the join was invisible.
And how he scolded when you wouldn't
leave the knife alone.

Oh, Benedict, you are hard. Whatever your rule
lays down as an edge, there are times
to lay it aside.

> *I pray,*
> *send evidence that this*
> *is one such time.*

. . .

Don't sulk.
You make me feel I got my way
with a child's tantrum. But I can't
make storms. It wasn't me who set
trees gnashing and the thunder growling.

Where is your peace? If God
has willed this weather, your abbey
won't capsize into sin with you gone
one night. Nor will any accuse you
of immorality with an old sister,
her neck wrapped in more shawls
than a sick giraffe.

Yes, that's more like your laugh.

Compline

This is the hour to stir the fire
and empty compline's cupboard
of prayers. The woods draw in. Branches
flog these faithful walls. Ancient trees
invoke the dark.

No, there's no-one out there.
The country people still avoid this place at night.
They call it sacred to the lady of beasts.

Oh, Benedict, it just takes time. You can't
excise the old beliefs like cancer. It's more
like being a gardener, watching how
the weeds come up, pinching them back.
Making a space for the true crop.

For even though you pulled Apollo's altar
down and built your chapel there, even though
converts sing your psalms and bless you
throughout the countryside ...

       Yes, I know
       they're the Lord's psalms, Benedict,
       not yours ...

still, folk will braid their superstitions
with their new beliefs, like the branches
interleaved around this hut.
When you describe for them the "bright armour
of obedience," they cannot help
but think of the old god's breastplate
and sun-gilt arrows.

Apollo had a sister too. His
twin, Artemis. Lady of the Beasts.
Folk still reverence her through all
this wild and mountainous region.
Virgin with her silver bow, huntress
and guardian of all pregnant creatures.

I am pregnant with death.
Succour me.

Vigiliae

The mid night prayers. Words
suddenly heavy. Narrow bedshelves
stand against the wall like biers.
Thanks be, I will not lie on one
tonight.

I have discovered I am afraid
of death. Absurdly
frightened. Do you know why?
I imagine my bones lying
paralyzed.
Desperate
to be re-joined.

Like an unstrung bow.
Or a marionette waiting
for the strings of resurrection.

This ugly thought weights
my soul down. And now death
waits so close.

. . .

Your words have a comfortable taste.
You were well named, Benedict – good-speaking.

Yes, you've helped. Don't look so worried.
I won't go to my coffin like a panicked pagan.
Won't disgrace the faith.

But keep the words coming. Tell me,
since the only the loaf of bread and I
will ever know the answer, what do you
fear?

Oh, don't be pious. God may
lend you courage. But he's not general
anaesthetic, a numb drug for doctors
of doctrine to prescribe. We're meant to be afraid,
sometimes, of the dark beyond the walls
the empty shelf, the knocking of fleshless
bones.

> *It's flesh you fear, I think.*
> *Women's flesh. The twin*
> *you cannot peel away.*
>
> *Although certainly you've tried.*
> *Only men may live in your*
> *thorn-rimmed community.*
> *Even my nuns and I a danger*
> *sequestered at an antiseptic distance.*

I always wondered who she was – the girl
whose memory frenzied you so much,
when you stripped and rolled your body
in thorns and nettles . . .

> . . . Why did I mention that?
> I hardly know. A mind often
> leaps sideways like game
> startled in a thicket . . .

You say you were never again
troubled in that way.   But you will never
tell me her name.

Lauds

Now come the prayers that lead to birdsong.
The wind, dropped
at last to its knees,
touches its lips to rain-heavy leaves.

This is the office of the day I love
most. It is a doubled benediction
that you are here to praise with me,
along with fruitful trees
and all cedars, mountains and all hills.

On this psalm-sweet morning,
I need to tell you
            brother
            twin
how I love you.

When you ran away, remember? A boy
yearning for ineffable perfection, slight
and ardent as a divining rod – when you ran
away, I was bereft.
The quiver of ideas we shared
rattled empty without you . . .

            . . . Yes, I know you had to go . . .

but still I felt abandoned,
            lost
as if tethered with pleasant beasts.

Love comes at a cost. Sometimes the price
is a gap in our lives, a space
in what might have been.

I have lain with no man, Benedict,
since we were coupled in the womb.
Will lie with none until your bones
come to wait in the same stone anteroom.

Was that a gap left empty, or a room I needed?
The virgin who drives off lovers
builds her own house in the grove

In a whole life, no other face
carved the same dear place in my heart.

. . . What am I saying, brother?

Only that
we are twins and I love you.
And for that love, have followed
as closely as I could, your footsteps
down the passages where God
cuts his inexplicable way.

. . .

Now. Give me the viaticum, the farewell
leaf of flour and water on my tongue.
Then go back to your monks.

Know that my love goes with you
always – a daily bread. A faint, green
heart-shaped thread
traced around the apple's core and seen
only when the whole is cut
apart.

68

AFTERWORD

It was the stories of women saints that pulled me in. Women do not make up the majority in the Oxford Dictionary of Saints, but there are still a substantial number. As I browsed, I started to notice patterns, stories that recurred. And the overarching pattern is that these saints almost never reflect the church-sanctioned role for a woman as wife and mother.

Women posing as men. Virgins who defied their families and friends and ran off. Abbesses who founded new rules and orders, women of political and administrative ability. Women who could do magic – float in the air, read hearts at a distance. It was as though certain ideas about how women should live their lives had been escorted firmly out the front door of the church only to climb in again through the back window.

There are stories to inspire a thousand books of poems. The ones I have used as the basis for this collection are mostly the shadowy ones, sometimes the wildly fantastical and clearly apocryphal. These were the tales that let me in. For instance, the legend about Saint Martha taming a dragon. Martha! That quintessential housewife with her traditional attributes of ladle and broom. How did a dragon come in?

For Martha – as for Marina, Pelagia, Catherine of Alexandria, Wilgefortis, Brigid, Anne, Xene, and Scholastica – the historical records are a faint trace or non-existent. There may be a passing reference in documents, around which a thicket of tale and oral tradition has grown up. In these cases, I felt relatively free to build my own hut from the twigs and branches.

However, four of the women in this book have more solid records. Eustochium of Padua, Veronica of Binasco, Louisa Albertoni, and Dorothea of Montau were all of the 14th and 15th centuries. None was officially canonized – they exist in a just-south-of-sainthood status as "Blesseds." The 'facts' that I used as starting points for each of their poems (such as Veronica crying a quart of tears, or Louisa baking her charitable coins into bread) were historically recorded incidents.

However, I haven't been able to track down the additional historical material that no doubt exists. In particular, I know there is a seven-volume life of the mystic, Dorothea of Montau, written in Latin. In that book, there must be information about her one surviving daughter who became a Benedictine nun, but I know nothing more than the bare fact that such a daughter existed. And the truth is, I didn't want to know much more. I had a story I wanted to tell about how the children of intensely idealistic parents can feel abandoned. I needed a saint with a biography a little like my own grandmother's. Dorothea filled the bill.

I took the bare bones of biographical events and built my own stories around them. I tried not to actively contradict what I knew to be historically the case. Dorothea's cell really did have three windows. Eustochium was indeed found with a cross burned on her chest after her death.

At the same time I know the real stories would be otherwise – here I mean 'stories' in the sense of the narrative that we each construct to describe and explain our lives. These monologues are not historical reconstruction. They are the narratives of a woman of my time and place – certainly not of a woman from 14th-century Prussia or first-century Palestine.

So I apologize to Dorothea's unnamed daughter and the others, who would have explained their lives quite otherwise.

OTHER BOOKS BY ALICE MAJOR:

Corona Radiata (2000)

Tales for an Urban Sky (1999)

Lattice of the Years (1998)

Time Travels Light (1992)

The Chinese Mirror (1988)